The True Story of
PAUL REVERE'S RIDE

Susanna Keller

PowerKiDS press

New York

To my parents, for encouraging my fascination with all the message-carrying little maids

Published in 2013 by The Rosen Publishing Group, Inc.
29 East 21st Street, New York, NY 10010

First Edition

Editor: Jennifer Way
Book Design: Colleen Bialecki

Photo Credits: Cover, p. 15 © Superstock/age fotostock; p. 5 Hulton Archive/Hulton Fine Art Collection/Getty Images; p. 7 English School/Private Collection/Peter Newark Military Pictures/The Bridgeman Art Library; p. 9 Jeffrey M. Frank/Shutterstock.com; p. 11 American School/Private Collection/Peter Newark American Pictures/The Bridgeman Art Library; p. 13 The Bridgeman Art Library/Getty Images; pp. 17, 21 jiawangkun/Shutterstock.com p. 19 © iStockphoto.com/S. Greg Panosian.

Library of Congress Cataloging-in-Publication Data

Keller, Susanna.
  The true story of Paul Revere's ride / by Susanna Keller. — 1st ed.
      p. cm. — (What really happened?)
  Includes index.
  ISBN 978-1-4488-9690-5 (library binding) — ISBN 978-1-4488-9838-1 (pbk.) —
  ISBN 978-1-4488-9839-8 (6-pack)
  1. Revere, Paul, 1735-1818—Juvenile literature. 2. Statesmen—Massachusetts—Biography—Juvenile literature. 3. Massachusetts—Biography—Juvenile literature. 4. Massachusetts—History—Revolution, 1775-1783—Juvenile literature. I. Title.
  F69.R43K45 2013
  974.4'03092—dc23
  [B]
                                    2012018697

Manufactured in the United States of America

CPSIA Compliance Information: Batch #W13PK4: For Further Information contact Rosen Publishing, New York, New York at 1-800-237-9932

CONTENTS

THE REAL RIDER

The story of Paul Revere's ride has been retold many times. On the night of April 18, 1775, Revere rode across the Massachusetts countryside warning people that British soldiers were coming. This helped the people of the Massachusetts Bay **Colony** win the Battles of Lexington and Concord. These were the first battles in the **American Revolution**. In this war, the people of what would become the United States won their freedom from Great Britain.

Revere was a real person. His famous ride really happened. However, it did not happen exactly as the stories tell. This book tells his true story.

Paul Revere became famous for his midnight ride but he was also a well-known silversmith and patriot in his Boston community.

A BOSTON BOY

Paul Revere was born in Boston, Massachusetts, on January 1, 1735. His father, Apollos Rivoire, came to Boston from France as a child. Rivoire changed his name to Revere because it was easier for people to say.

Paul's father was a goldsmith. He taught Paul to make things from fine metals. In time, Paul became a successful silversmith.

Paul fought in the **French and Indian War**, which lasted from 1754 until 1763. In this war, the British, the French, and the Native American groups that sided with each fought over parts of North America.

The French and Indian War is also known as the Seven Years' War. This painting shows the Battle of the Monongahela, in today's Pennsylvania.

SILVERSMITH AND MORE

In 1757, Revere married Sarah Orne. They had eight children together. She died in 1773. Later that year, he married Rachel Walker. They had eight children, too!

Revere worked hard to support his big family. As a silversmith, he made silver spoons, buckles, teapots, and more. He worked with gold, too. He also **engraved** copper plates. These were used to print drawings. Revere even made false teeth and worked as a dentist for a while!

Revere was a trusted member of his community. He joined many community groups. He was on the **committee** that brought in Boston's first streetlights.

Paul Revere's house in Boston, shown here, is still standing today.

LIFE IN THE COLONIES

In 1763, the British won the French and Indian War. At that time, Massachusetts, where Revere lived, was one of several British colonies in North America. Colonies are places people have moved to that are still ruled by the leaders of the country from which they came.

The French and Indian War was expensive. To help pay for it, the British government passed laws that taxed many things colonists bought. For example, the Stamp Act taxed paper goods. The laws made many colonists mad. The British government also passed laws that put limits on Colonial governments. These taxes and laws made many colonists angry.

This 1766 engraving was created to celebrate British Parliament's repeal, or ending, of the Stamp Act. It was passed in 1765 and repealed in 1766.

A SON OF LIBERTY

Revere joined groups that fought for colonists' rights, such as the **Sons of Liberty**. On December 16, 1773, members of this group dumped a shipload of tea into Boston's harbor to protest the British tax on tea. This event is known as the Boston Tea Party.

Revere knew that the British soldiers in Boston feared an uprising and planned to capture the colonists' arms and gunpowder. In December 1774, he rode to Portsmouth, New Hampshire, to warn townspeople. However, the British did not arrive until several days later. When they got there, they discovered the townspeople had captured the fort and taken the supplies!

This picture shows the Sons of Liberty throwing tea into Boston Harbor during the Boston Tea Party.

THE FAMOUS RIDE

On April 18, 1775, Joseph Warren told Revere that the British were sending soldiers to Lexington to arrest Colonial leaders John Hancock and Samuel Adams. Revere slipped out of Boston by boat. He landed in Charlestown, Massachusetts, and borrowed a horse to ride to Lexington. Along the way, he told people about the soldiers' plans. After reaching Lexington, he headed to Concord, where colonists stored supplies.

Revere's warning let Hancock and Adams escape. It also gave Colonial **militias** time to gather. When the British reached Lexington **Common**, fighting broke out. The British pushed through to Concord, but the colonists eventually pushed the British back to Boston.

Revere warned everyone he saw on the way to Lexington that soldiers were coming.

WHICH PARTS ARE TRUE?

Revere wasn't the only rider that night. Though Revere got there first, William Dawes also carried the news from Boston to Lexington. On the way to Concord, Revere and Dawes ran into Samuel Prescott. Then, a group of British soldiers captured them. Only Prescott escaped to warn Concord.

Stories get other details wrong, too. Some say Revere waited in Charlestown for lanterns to be hung in Boston's Old North Church to learn if the British were coming by land or sea. By that point, Revere knew they were coming by sea. The lanterns were a backup plan in case he got caught.

Here is the Old North Church (center). There are many more buildings here today than in Revere's Boston!

REVERE IN THE REVOLUTION

Though Revere was captured before reaching Concord, he soon convinced the British to free him. As fighting broke out on Lexington Common, Revere helped move a trunk of important papers from a **tavern** in which the British could have captured it.

After the Battles of Lexington and Concord, Revere carried word of the militia's win to other colonies. This convinced many colonists to join the fight against Britain. Others, known as **Loyalists**, sided with the British.

Revere joined the army in 1776. In 1779, he took part in the Penobscot Expedition, in which the American **Navy** failed to drive the British from the Penobscot peninsula.

The Penobscot Expedition was the largest American naval expedition during the American Revolution. This picture shows Penobscot Bay, in today's Maine.

AFTER THE WAR

The British surrendered in 1781, ending the fighting. In 1783, the two countries signed a peace **treaty**. Revere returned to his silversmith business. In 1788, he opened a **foundry**, or place where metal is cast. It made cannons, bells, and parts for ships. Some of his bells are still used today. In 1801, he opened the first American copper-rolling mill. Revere died in Boston on May 10, 1818.

In 1860, Henry Wadsworth Longfellow published a poem called "Paul Revere's Ride." It made Revere famous throughout the United States. This poem contained some of the misunderstandings about the event that became part of Paul Revere's legend.

Paul Revere was the first American to roll copper into sheets. In 1802, his copper sheets were used to cover the dome of the Massachusetts Statehouse, shown here.

WHAT REALLY HAPPENED?

There are many records of Paul Revere's ride and the events leading up to it. However, the story often gets simplified. Historical truths are often stretched or lost when they are retold as novels, movies, or in a poem, as in Paul Revere's case. Revere was one of several Colonial leaders who guessed the British were up to something and warned their fellow colonists.

Like most events, this one involved many people. While Dawes and Prescott helped Revere spread the news to Lexington and Concord, other riders carried it to other towns. Revere played a key role, but he did not play it alone!

GLOSSARY

American Revolution (uh-MER-uh-ken reh-vuh-LOO-shun) Battles that soldiers from the colonies fought against Britain for freedom, from 1775 to 1783.

colony (KAH-luh-nee) A new place where people move that is still ruled by the leaders of the country from which they came.

committee (kuh-MIH-tee) A group of people directed to oversee or consider a matter.

common (KAH-mun) An open area in a town or city not owned by any one person, much like a park today.

engraved (en-GRAYVD) Carved into.

foundry (FOWN-dree) A place where metal is melted and shaped.

French and Indian War (FRENCH AND IN-dee-un WOR) The battles fought between 1754 and 1763 by England, France, and Native Americans for control of North America.

Loyalists (LOY-uh-lists) People who were faithful to the British Crown during the American Revolution.

militias (muh-LIH-shuz) Groups of people who are trained and ready to fight when needed.

navy (NAY-vee) A group of sailors who are trained to fight at sea.

Sons of Liberty (SUNZ UV LIH-ber-tee) A group of American colonists who were Whigs and who protested the British government's taxes and unfair treatment before the American Revolution.

tavern (TA-vurn) A place to spend the night and eat a meal.

treaty (TREE-tee) An official agreement, signed and agreed upon by each party.

INDEX

WEBSITES

Due to the changing nature of Internet links, PowerKids Press has developed an online list of websites related to the subject of this book. This site is updated regularly. Please use this link to access the list:
www.powerkidslinks.com/wrh/revere/